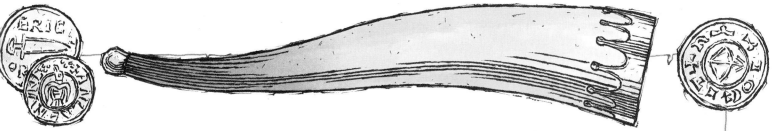

# THE FACTS ABOUT

# THE VIKINGS

Dereen Taylor

**WAYLAND**

First published in Great Britain in 1994 by Simon
and Schuster Young Books
Reprinted by Macdonald Young Books in 1997 as
*What Do We Know About the Vikings*
by Hazel Mary Martell
This differentiated text edition by Dereen Taylor,
published in 2007 by Wayland
Copyright © Wayland 2007
All rights reserved.

Wayland
338 Euston Road
London NW1 3BH

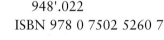
Wayland Australia
Level 17/207 Kent Street
Sydney, NSW 2000

Original series design: David West
Illustrator: Rob Shone
Layout for this edition: Jane Hawkins
Editor for this edition: Katie Powell

British Library Cataloguing in Publication Data

Taylor, Dereen
  Facts about the Vikings
  1. Vikings - Juvenile literature
  I. Title II. The Vikings
  948'.022
ISBN 978 0 7502 5260 7

Printed in China
Wayland is a division of Hachette Children's Books, an Hachette Livre UK company.

Picture acknowledgements: Cover front: Michael Holford; WF/Statens Historiska Museum, Stockholm;
Aalborg Historiske Museum: 13(t); Courtesy, Canadian Parks Service: p38; Martyn F. Chillmaid: p14,
p15(b), p16; C.M. Dixon: p17(r), p20, p26(b), p28, p31, p40; Forhistorisk Museum, Moesgard: p19;
Werner Forman Archive: p7, p9, p17(1), p30; WF/National Museum, Copenhagen: p33(t), p34(b),
WF/Statens Historiska Museum, Stockholm: p26(t), p32; WF/Stofnun Arnamagnussonar, Iceland:p33(b);
WF/Viking Ships Museum, Bygdy, Oslo: p36-37; Robert Harding Picture Library: p8(t), p14, p29(1);
Michael Holford: endpapers, p12-13, p22(b), p25(b), p29(r), p37(b), p39(b), p40(1), p41, p42; National
Museum of Ireland, Dublin: p22(t); Skyggna Myndverk: p18(b); Statens Historiska Museum: p15(t);
Stofnun Arnamagnussonar, Iceland: p12(t), p31(t); Universitetets Oldsaksamling, Oslo: p34-35, p37(t);
David Williams: p18(t), p39(t); York Archaeological Trust Picture Library, p8(b), p21, p23, p24, p25(t),
p35(b), p40(r).

Endpapers: This viking carving was excavated from St Paul's Churchyard, London. It shows a battle
between a lion and a serpent and dates from around AD 1030. It stands 18 inches high and was set up
by two Vikings called Ginna and Toki.

# CONTENTS

Words that appear in **bold** can be found in the glossary on page 44.

# WHO WERE THE VIKINGS?

Look at the two maps on page 9. The small map shows the countries the Vikings came from. The large map shows the places they went to between AD 780 and 1100. This period is called the Viking Age. The Vikings were fierce fighters who raided towns and **monasteries**. The Vikings were also great adventurers. They travelled looking for new lands where they could settle down and farm.

## ▶ THE VIKING HOMELANDS

By the end of the eighth century, the Vikings wanted to leave Scandinavia to find new land to farm. As this photograph of Norway shows, there are lots of mountains in Norway. This made it difficult to find good farmland.

## ▼ METAL WORKERS

The Vikings melted the ore and made metal. Then they made the metal into cooking pans, hammerheads and axes. Skilled metal workers made swords like the one below.

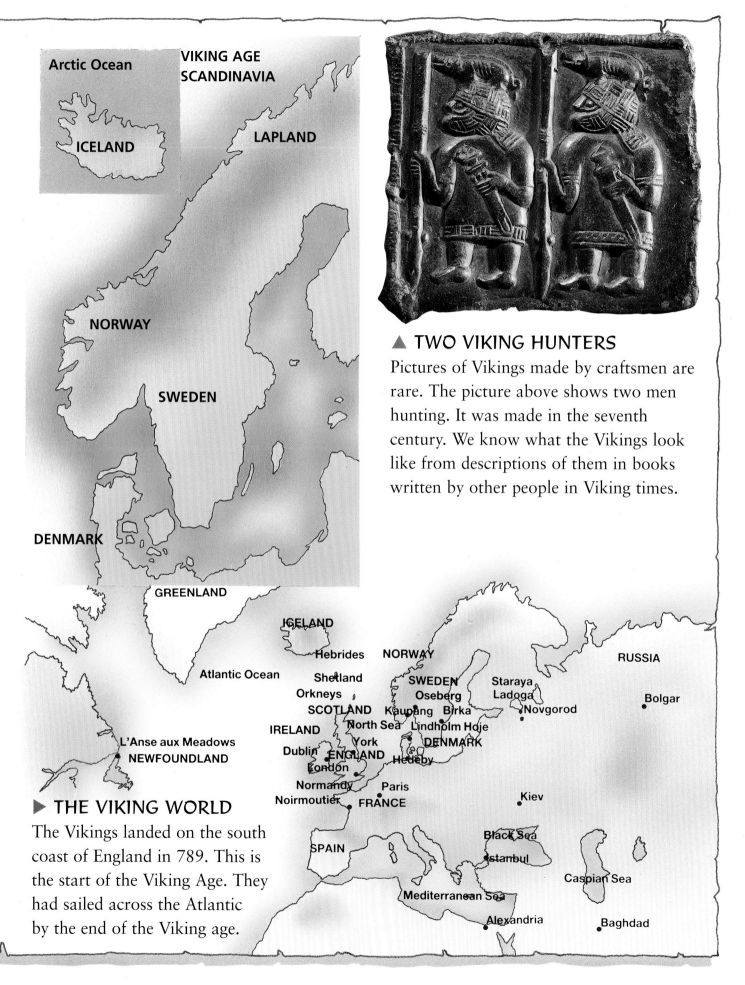

Arctic Ocean

**VIKING AGE SCANDINAVIA**

ICELAND

LAPLAND

NORWAY

SWEDEN

DENMARK

GREENLAND

ICELAND

Hebrides

NORWAY

RUSSIA

Atlantic Ocean

Shetland

Orkneys

SCOTLAND

IRELAND

SWEDEN

Oseberg

Kaupang  Birka

North Sea  Lindholm Hoje

Staraya
Ladoga

Novgorod

Bolgar

L'Anse aux Meadows
NEWFOUNDLAND

York

Dublin  ENGLAND

London

Normandy

Noirmoutier  FRANCE

Paris

DENMARK

Hedeby

Kiev

Black Sea

SPAIN

Istanbul

Caspian Sea

Mediterranean Sea

Alexandria

Baghdad

## ▲ TWO VIKING HUNTERS

Pictures of Vikings made by craftsmen are rare. The picture above shows two men hunting. It was made in the seventh century. We know what the Vikings look like from descriptions of them in books written by other people in Viking times.

## ▶ THE VIKING WORLD

The Vikings landed on the south coast of England in 789. This is the start of the Viking Age. They had sailed across the Atlantic by the end of the Viking age.

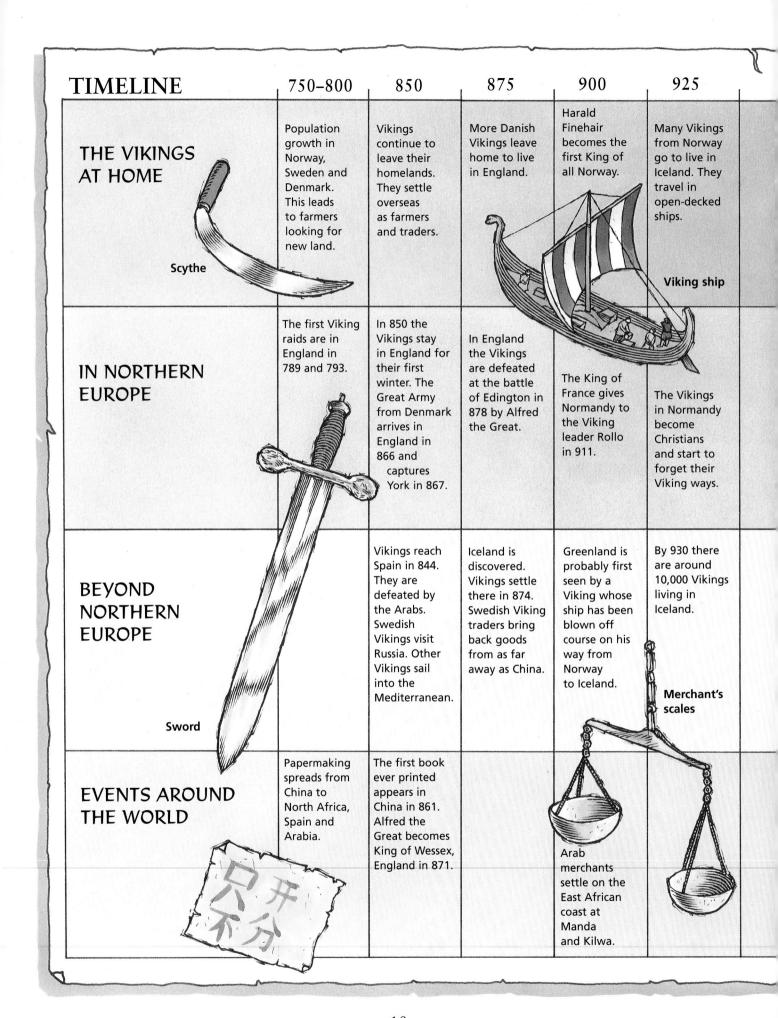

| TIMELINE | 750–800 | 850 | 875 | 900 | 925 |
|---|---|---|---|---|---|
| **THE VIKINGS AT HOME** | Population growth in Norway, Sweden and Denmark. This leads to farmers looking for new land. | Vikings continue to leave their homelands. They settle overseas as farmers and traders. | More Danish Vikings leave home to live in England. | Harald Finehair becomes the first King of all Norway. | Many Vikings from Norway go to live in Iceland. They travel in open-decked ships. |
| **IN NORTHERN EUROPE** | The first Viking raids are in England in 789 and 793. | In 850 the Vikings stay in England for their first winter. The Great Army from Denmark arrives in England in 866 and captures York in 867. | In England the Vikings are defeated at the battle of Edington in 878 by Alfred the Great. | The King of France gives Normandy to the Viking leader Rollo in 911. | The Vikings in Normandy become Christians and start to forget their Viking ways. |
| **BEYOND NORTHERN EUROPE** | | Vikings reach Spain in 844. They are defeated by the Arabs. Swedish Vikings visit Russia. Other Vikings sail into the Mediterranean. | Iceland is discovered. Vikings settle there in 874. Swedish Viking traders bring back goods from as far away as China. | Greenland is probably first seen by a Viking whose ship has been blown off course on his way from Norway to Iceland. | By 930 there are around 10,000 Vikings living in Iceland. |
| **EVENTS AROUND THE WORLD** | Papermaking spreads from China to North Africa, Spain and Arabia. | The first book ever printed appears in China in 861. Alfred the Great becomes King of Wessex, England in 871. | | Arab merchants settle on the East African coast at Manda and Kilwa. | |

Scythe

Viking ship

Sword

Merchant's scales

开
只 分
不

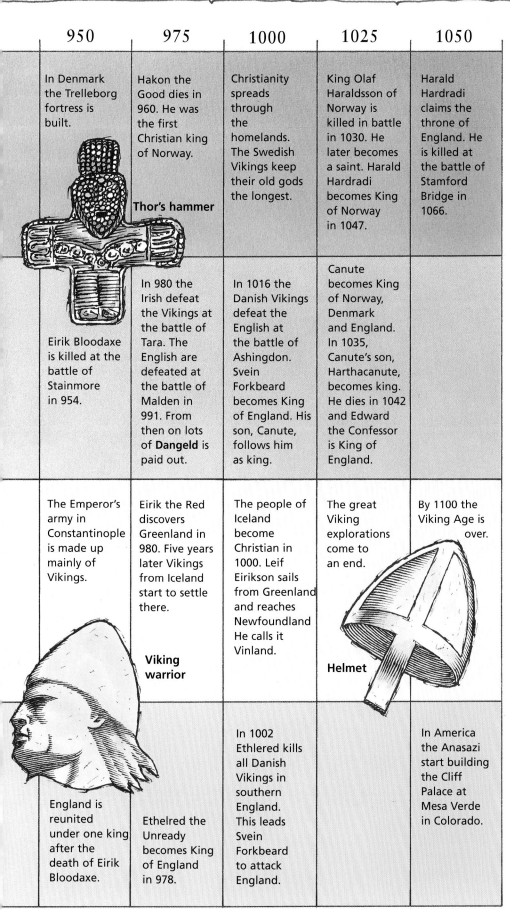

| 950 | 975 | 1000 | 1025 | 1050 |
|---|---|---|---|---|
| In Denmark the Trelleborg fortress is built. | Hakon the Good dies in 960. He was the first Christian king of Norway. **Thor's hammer** | Christianity spreads through the homelands. The Swedish Vikings keep their old gods the longest. | King Olaf Haraldsson of Norway is killed in battle in 1030. He later becomes a saint. Harald Hardradi becomes King of Norway in 1047. | Harald Hardradi claims the throne of England. He is killed at the battle of Stamford Bridge in 1066. |
| Eirik Bloodaxe is killed at the battle of Stainmore in 954. | In 980 the Irish defeat the Vikings at the battle of Tara. The English are defeated at the battle of Malden in 991. From then on lots of **Dangeld** is paid out. | In 1016 the Danish Vikings defeat the English at the battle of Ashingdon. Svein Forkbeard becomes King of England. His son, Canute, follows him as king. | Canute becomes King of Norway, Denmark and England. In 1035, Canute's son, Harthacanute, becomes king. He dies in 1042 and Edward the Confessor is King of England. | |
| The Emperor's army in Constantinople is made up mainly of Vikings. | Eirik the Red discovers Greenland in 980. Five years later Vikings from Iceland start to settle there. **Viking warrior** | The people of Iceland become Christian in 1000. Leif Eirikson sails from Greenland and reaches Newfoundland He calls it Vinland. | The great Viking explorations come to an end. **Helmet** | By 1100 the Viking Age is over. |
| England is reunited under one king after the death of Eirik Bloodaxe. | Ethelred the Unready becomes King of England in 978. | In 1002 Ethlered kills all Danish Vikings in southern England. This leads Svein Forkbeard to attack England. | | In America the Anasazi start building the Cliff Palace at Mesa Verde in Colorado. |

# THE AGE OF MIGRATIONS

The Viking Age came near the end of the Age of Migrations. This was a long period of time when many people were on the move across Europe. It started around the fifth century AD. Sailors crossed the North Sea and attacked Britain. At the same time, the Roman Empire was collapsing. Roman soldiers left Britain to defend Rome. When they had gone, **Angles**, **Jutes**, **Frisians** and **Anglo-Saxons** moved to England. At the end of the eighth century, the Vikings left their homelands. They were looking for treasure, land and trade in these new kingdoms.

# THE LAST VIKING KINGS

In 1066 Harald Hardradi became King of England. He was killed at the Battle of Stamford Bridge.

11

# DID THE VIKINGS GROW THEIR OWN FOOD?

Most Vikings were farmers who grew their own food. They usually had small farms and grew just enough food to feed their own families. In their

fields they grew grain crops including oats, barley, wheat and rye. They also grew vegetables such as cabbages, onions and beans. They kept geese and goats, as well as sheep, cattle, pigs and hens.

## ▲ FISHING

Nearly all Viking farms were near the sea. Most Vikings went fishing to catch cod or herring. They used a net or a hook on a line. Some fishermen speared fish from a boat. The fishermen in the picture above have caught a whale.

## ▼ FARMING

The picture below is from the Bayeux Tapestry. The tapestry was made at the end of the Viking Age. It shows how the Vikings farmed. First the land was ploughed, then the seeds were scattered by hand. A horse-drawn **harrow** then covered the seeds with soil.

## ▶ A PLOUGHED FIELD

A lot of the Viking farmland is still farmed today. This means that the signs of Viking farming have gone. But some farms were not used after the Viking Age. In the centre of this photograph you can see part of a ploughed field from Viking times.

## ▶ MAKING FLOUR

The Vikings made flour using two stones. One stone was twisted on top of the other until the grain between the stones had been ground into flour.

## ▼ FARM TOOLS

Viking farmers used horses to pull ploughs and harrows. All the other work was done by hand. They used long-handled scythes to cut hay and sickles to cut grain crops. Hoes were used for weeding and spades for digging.

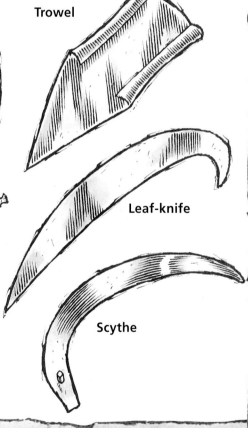

Trowel

Leaf-knife

Scythe

## THE VIKING SUMMER

Spring was a busy time on the farm. Fields were ploughed and seeds were sown in the ground. Manure was spread on the hayfields to make the grass grow.

The farmer then probably went raiding or trading for the summer. His family would look after the farm. The farmer came back for the harvest at the end of summer.

# DID THE VIKINGS GO SHOPPING?

Most Vikings lived in small settlements with no shops. They made most of the things they needed. These included clothes, tools and furniture. But some

towns became **trading centres**. The main ones were Hedeby in Denmark, Birka in Sweden, Kaupang in Norway and Jorvik (York) in England. In these towns the Vikings could buy silk, glassware and wine.

## ▼ POTS AND PLATES

This photograph shows **reconstructions** of Viking pottery, wooden plates and bowls. The reconstructions are based on pieces found by **archaeologists** in York, in a street called Coppergate.

This name probably comes from two Viking words – Koppr, which means cup and gat which means street. Most Viking cups and plates were made from wood. Clay cups and plates were more unusual.

## ▶ HACK SILVER

Sometimes the early Vikings exchanged their goods for silver finger-rings and arm-rings. When they needed money, they cut pieces of silver off the rings. The silver was weighed on scales and used as money.

## ◀ THE SHOPS AT JORVIK

This picture shows a Viking workshop which has been rebuilt at the Jorvik Museum in York. This shop belonged to a leather worker. He made shoes, belts and harnesses for horses.

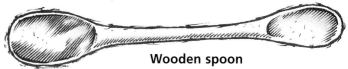

**Wooden spoon**

## ▼ MAKING A COIN

Coins were hand-made by a moneyer. He engraved one side of the coin backwards on a metal die (1). Then he put the **die** on a strip of silver (2) and tapped it with a hammer to make an imprint. He made a row of imprints on one side of the strip (3). Then he split the coins (4). He stamped the other side of the coin with a different die.

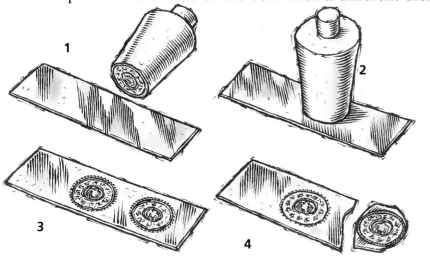

## 🥾 EVIDENCE 🎲

We know about the things sold in Viking shops from the objects dug up by archaeologists. In York they could only dig up a small area as the site of Jorvik has been built over many times since the Viking Age. But in Denmark and Sweden the old market towns of Hedeby and Birka had been abandoned. At both these sites archaeologists found bits of glassware and pieces of silk. They also found everyday things, such as pins, needles and spoons.

# DID THE VIKINGS HAVE FAMILIES LIKE OURS?

A Viking's family included parents and children and also cousins, aunts and uncles. Grandparents, parents and children often lived together in the same house. The Vikings thought that loyalty to the family was more

important than loyalty to a leader. If someone was murdered, his family would murder someone from the killer's family. The two families could then be at war with each other for many years.

## ▲ THE FAMILY AT HOME

The fireplace was the most important place in the Viking home. The fire gave heat and light and food was cooked over it. This photograph of actors dressed as Vikings shows how the whole family would gather round the fireplace.

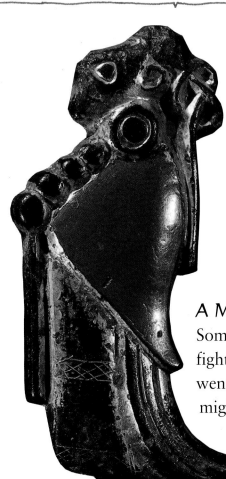

## ◀ VIKING WOMEN

This pendant on the left shows a Viking woman. Women were treated well. They could choose their own husband or stay single if they wanted to. If a woman's husband was away, the woman was left in charge of the house and business.

## A MEMORIAL STONE ▶

Some Vikings were killed in fights or accidents when they went off raiding. Their families might put up a carved stone to remember them. This stone is from Sweden.

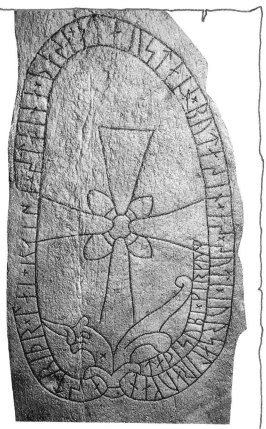

## ▼ USEFUL TOOLS

Viking clothes did not have pockets. Instead, Vikings carried the things they needed on a chain hanging from a brooch. These things included needles made out of fine bones. A woman also carried a knife, scissors and keys to any chests in the house.

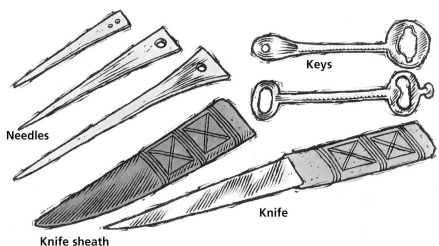

Needles

Keys

Knife

Knife sheath

##  MARRIAGE

Viking men and women could choose who they wanted to marry. They did not need permission from their parents. Most marriages took place in the early winter, when everyone was at home. The marriage was celebrated with a big feast shared by family, friends and neighbours. The celebrations included eating and drinking and also poetry, music and dancing. The occasion could last as long as two weeks. If the marriage did not work, it was very easy for the Viking couple to get a divorce.

# DID THE VIKINGS LIVE IN HOUSES?

Most Viking families lived on farms in the country. Their houses were known as longhouses, because of their shape. Often Viking houses had only one large room or hall. Everyone ate and slept in this room. Sometimes the barn for the animals was built on to the end of the house. Only a small number of Vikings lived in towns.

## ◀ ▼ THE FARMHOUSE AT STONG

There are few Viking houses left today because the houses were usually built out of wood, which rots. But a farmhouse at Stong in Iceland was dug up by **archaeologists** in 1939. There was enough of the building left to make the **reconstruction** below. The walls were made of blocks of turf, as shown on the left.

## FURNITURE ▶

The Vikings did not have much furniture. Only the farmer and his wife slept on a bed. Everyone else slept on a raised ledge along the wall of the room. Spare clothes and blankets were kept in chests.

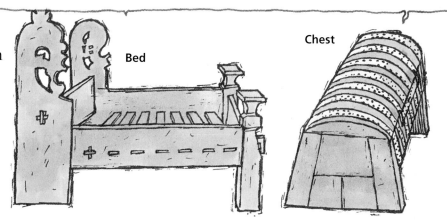

Bed

Chest

## ▼ KITCHEN UTENSILS

Vikings ate lots of dairy products made with the help of butter churns and cheese drainers. They stored food in wooden tubs. Flour often had bits of stone in it. These came from the stones used to grind the grain. The bits of stone wore the Vikings' teeth down!

Wooden tub

Knife

Wooden bowls

Cheese drainer

## ▼ INSIDE A HOUSE

This reconstruction in Denmark shows the inside of a Viking house. The fireplace is in the middle of the room. A cooking pot is hanging from a chain from the roof. On the right of the door is the bed.

## EATING MEALS

Vikings usually ate two meals a day. The first meal was eaten at eight o'clock in the morning and the second meal at seven o'clock at night. They used folding tables that were set up especially for meal times. Food was eaten from wooden bowls or plates. There were knives and spoons, but no forks.

# WHO WENT TO WORK IN THE VIKING LANDS?

Most Vikings were freemen who owned their own land and worked for themselves. Their wives and children helped with the work. Some Vikings were slaves. They did heavy work like digging up **iron ore**. Some Vikings were traders as well as farmers and some were craftsmen who made jewellery and weapons.

◀ MAKING A SWORD

This woodcarving shows a scene from the legend of Sigurd the Dragon-slayer. Sigurd and another Viking warrior called Reginn are making a sword. Sigurd works the bellows to keep the fire hot while Reginn hammers the blade of the sword flat.

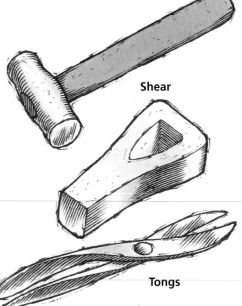

Hammer

Shear

Tongs

▶ BLACKSMITH'S TOOLS

A Viking **blacksmith** used tools very much like those used today. His hammer had an iron head fixed onto a wooden handle. He smoothed rough edges of metal with a shear like the one on the right. He used iron tongs to bend hot metal into shape.

## ▼ ▶ MAKING BEADS

Craftsmen made beads from jet, amber and crystal. They also made beads out of glass, like the ones shown here. The Vikings melted the glass in small pots and pulled it into long sticks. The sticks were then wrapped around a metal rod. When the sticks hardened, the rod was taken out and the glass cut into beads. Glass sticks of different colours could be twisted together to make patterned beads.

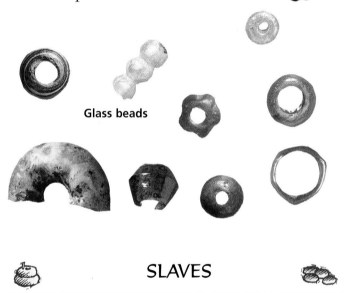

**Glass beads**

## ▼ MAKING A COMB

The Vikings made their combs from pieces of deer antler (1). They cut a long strip of antler (2) and split it into two pieces along its length. This was for the top of the comb. They cut oblong pieces (3) which were slotted between the two long pieces and fixed together with nails. The oblong pieces were then sawed into teeth (4). A pattern was often made along the top of the comb.

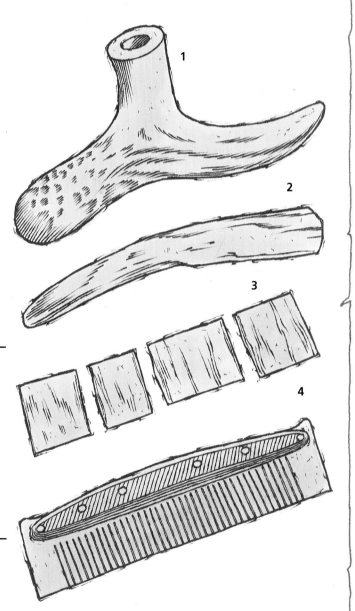

## SLAVES

There were three groups of slaves. The first group was made up of the children of slaves. The second group was prisoners taken in battle. The third group was people who had volunteered to become slaves so that they had food and somewhere to live. Slaves had no rights and no property. But a slave could work very hard and buy freedom for himself and his family.

# WHAT DID THE VIKINGS DO ON THEIR HOLIDAYS?

The Vikings did not go away on holiday. But they did have three religious celebrations a year. These were Sigrblot in the summer, Vetrarblot after the harvest and Jolablot after midwinter. At other times the Vikings relaxed by ice-skating, wrestling, swimming and hunting.

## ▶ GAMES AND SKILLS

In bad weather Vikings enjoyed playing board games. Some were played on boards like the one on the right. In good weather they played a sort of football. They also had rowing races and wrestling matches. Another test was to see who could walk all the way round a longship by balancing on its oars as the boat was being rowed.

## ◀ CHESS

The three chessmen on the left are from a set found on the Isle of Lewis in the Hebrides. They were carved in the twelfth century. Other Viking board games included hnefatafl. This had one playing piece like a king and the others pieces were plain. It is likely the king had to be defended from pieces on the other side.

## ▶ ICE-SKATING

When the rivers froze, the Vikings went skating. Skates were made from the foot bones of cattle and horses. They made a hole in the skate and stuck a peg in it. It was then tied to the shoe.

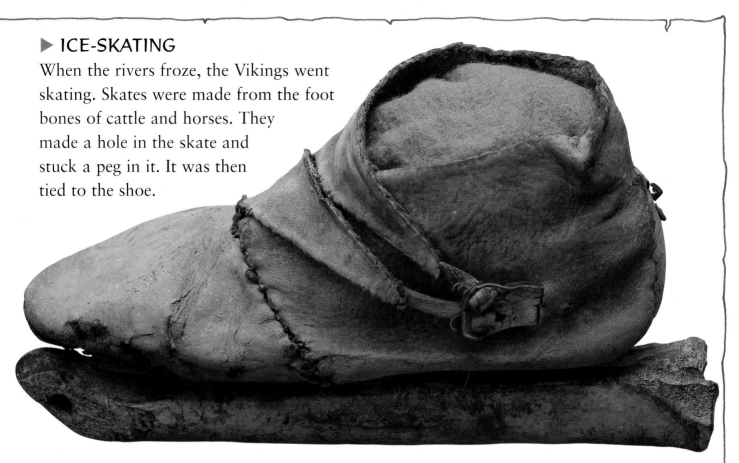

## ▶ PLAYING PIECES

The Vikings used playing pieces made from wood, stone, ivory and glass for their board games. These pieces are based on ones found in Birka.

## ▼ DRINKING HORNS

Viking feasts could last for two weeks and involved a lot of drinking. The Vikings brewed beer and a drink called mead. They drank from horns like the one below.

**Gambling pieces**

**Drinking horn**

## SACRIFICES

At the three religious feasts a horse was **sacrificed** to the gods. If the horse was killed, the meat from it was cooked and eaten by the Vikings. But sacrificed horses were not always killed. If the horse lived, the Viking shared the horse with the gods. It stayed with the Viking while it was useful to him. Then when the horse died, it belonged to the gods. We do not think that the Vikings sacrificed people.

# WHAT DID THE VIKINGS WEAR?

Viking men wore tunics and tight-fitting trousers. Women wore long dresses made of linen, that had a woollen tunic over the top. Everyone wore flat leather shoes, cloaks in cold weather and jewellery. Pieces of Viking clothing have been dug up by **archaeologists**.

## A VIKING FISHERMAN ▼

This model of a fisherman is in the Jorvik Museum. His head and face are the same size as those of a real Viking skull.

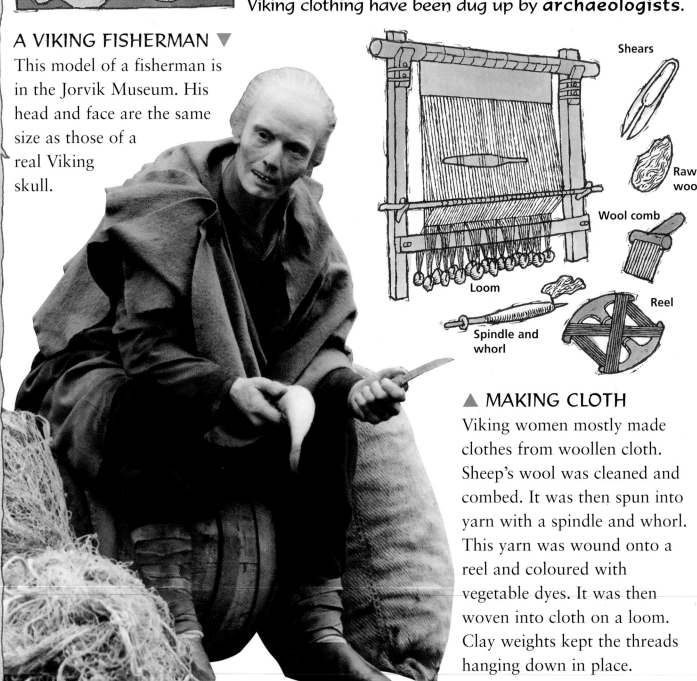

Shears

Raw wool

Wool comb

Loom

Spindle and whorl

Reel

## ▲ MAKING CLOTH

Viking women mostly made clothes from woollen cloth. Sheep's wool was cleaned and combed. It was then spun into yarn with a spindle and whorl. This yarn was wound onto a reel and coloured with vegetable dyes. It was then woven into cloth on a loom. Clay weights kept the threads hanging down in place.

## SHOES ▶

To make a shoe Vikings used a last like the one on the right. It was made of wood and shaped like a foot. The leather shoe was made around the last. Most shoes were held on to the wearer's foot with a leather strip. Sometimes farmers made their own shoes but there were also shoemakers in towns.

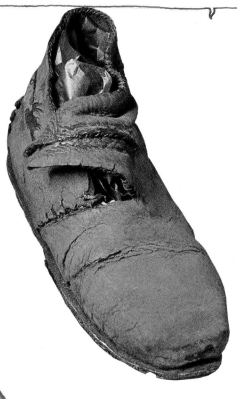

Last

Tortoise brooches

## ▲ BROOCHES

The Vikings fastened their clothes with belts or brooches. The brooches, shown above were called tortoise brooches because of their shape. They had a pin underneath and Viking women threaded this pin through a long loop at the back of their tunics. It then went through a shorter loop at the front. A string of beads showed how wealthy a family was. Both men and women used large pins to fasten their cloaks in winter.

## HYGIENE

It is hard to know whether the Vikings were clean or dirty. Men in England complained about their women liking the Vikings who combed their hair, bathed and changed their clothes so often! But an Arab who wrote about the Vikings said they did not wash often enough. Because lots of combs have been found, it seems that the Vikings took care of their hair. Men fastened their hair back with a band. They kept their beards and moustaches neatly trimmed. Married women covered their hair with a scarf.

# WHO DID THE VIKINGS WORSHIP?

The early Vikings had many different gods and goddesses. They thought the gods lived in a place called Asgard. The Vikings themselves lived in Midgard and beyond this was Utgard where the Frost Giants lived. They believed that one day the Frost Giants would destroy all the gods, bringing the world to an end.

Loki

## ODIN AND LOKI ▲▼

Odin was the most important Viking god. He was the wise god of poets and the god of kings and warriors. Legends said that Loki, the mischief-maker, once had his lips sewn together as a punishment.

Odin

## ◀ STAVE CHURCHES

There are still some ancient churches in Scandinavia. This one is at Borgund in Norway. They are called stave churches because their walls are made of upright planks of wood, called staves. By the time they were built, the Viking Age was over. The people of the Viking lands had become Christians.

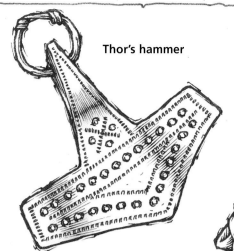

Thor's hammer

## ▼ MAKING THOR'S HAMMER

The craftsman made a model of the hammer in wax (1). He pressed the model in clay to make a mould (2). The mould was heated to melt the wax. It ran out of a hole and left the shape of the hammer behind (3). Melted silver was poured into the mould. When it was hard, the silver hammer was taken out (4).

1.

2.

3.

4.

## ▲ THOR AND HIS HAMMER

Thor was the most popular Viking god. He was thought to be a huge man with a red beard. He made thunder rumble by riding across the sky in a chariot pulled by goats. Thor was not as clever as Odin. He had to use a hammer as a weapon in his battles with the giants. Many Vikings wore a small copy of this hammer. They thought it would protect them from bad luck.

## HOW THE VIKINGS BECAME CHRISTIANS

The Vikings who travelled were the first to become Christians. This was because it was easier to trade with Christian merchants if they shared the same religion. But Christianity did not spread widely until the late Viking Age. The Vikings in

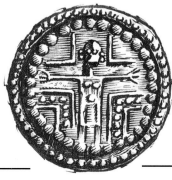

Iceland voted on religion in AD 1000. Half of them voted to become Christians. The other half voted to keep worshipping the old gods. Christianity finally won, but people could still worship the old gods in secret.

# DID THE VIKINGS BELIEVE IN LIFE AFTER DEATH?

Viking warriors thought that if they died in battle, they would go to a place called Valhalla. There they would be able to kill each other all day long. In the evening they would go back to Odin's hall and come back to life again. After feasting, they would be ready to fight again the next morning. But if Vikings died in bed, they would go to a cold, frosty place.

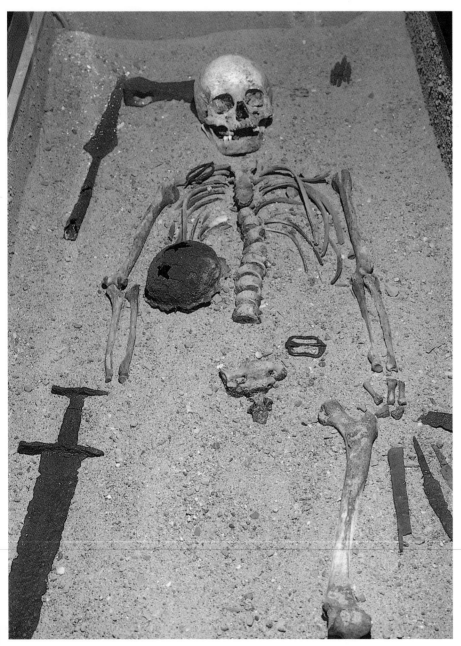

### ◀ GRAVE GOODS

Men and women were given **grave goods** for their journey to the next life. This Viking warrior's grave was dug up in Norway. Only part of the warrior's skeleton was left. His sword was by his right hand and pieces of his shield were on his chest. A dead warrior was given food and drink for the journey to Valhalla. Traders were often buried with some of the goods they traded.

**Grave goods**

## THE JOURNEY TO VALHALLA ▶

On the right is a picture stone from Sweden. It shows how warriors who die in battle go to Valhalla. The bottom picture shows them travelling there in a longship. The top picture shows a warrior arriving at Valhalla. He has been brought back to life and given a horse. He is being offered a drink before going to the feast in Odin's hall.

## ▲ STONE SHIPS

Important Vikings were buried in their ships, but most Vikings were buried in ordinary graves. These were often marked with stones in the shape of a ship. The photograph above shows a grave in Denmark.

## CREMATION

Not all Vikings were buried. Some were burnt or **cremated**. A Viking **chieftain** was cremated at the river Volga in 922. First, wood was piled up on the riverbank. Then the chieftain's ship was lifted on top of the wood and his body was carried on board the ship.

Food and drink for the dead man included two cows and a cockerel. A slave girl was **sacrificed** on board. The chieftain's men watched as the wood was set alight. When everything had burned, the ashes were placed in a special grave. This was called a memorial mound.

# WHO RULED THE VIKINGS?

The early Vikings had no rulers. The local government, called a **Thing**, set the laws. Freemen had the right to vote in the Thing. The most powerful man in an area became the leader, or jarl. Jarls, also known as kings, only ruled a small area. Later kings ruled Denmark, Norway and Sweden.

## THINGVELLIR ▼

Iceland did not have a king during the Viking Age. Instead, the people were ruled by two Things. The lower Thing looked after local issues. The higher level was the Althing. This met at Thingvellir, which is shown in the photograph. The Althing met for two weeks at midsummer every year. Only the men could vote, but they took their families to Thingvellir with them.

Most Vikings obeyed the laws of the Things. Anyone who did not, became an outlaw. An outlaw had to give up all his land and leave the country as quickly as possible. This was because anyone could kill an outlaw without being punished. Eirik the Red was outlawed from Norway in 980. He went to Iceland but was soon outlawed there too.

## ▲ THE KING OF NORWAY

The picture above is from a book called the Flateyjarbok. It shows Harald Finehair, the first king to rule over Norway.

**Coins of Viking kings**

## ▶ JEWELLING STONE

The stone on the right was set up in Jelling in Denmark. It has three sides. The one you can see here shows an imaginary animal with a snake wrapped round its body. The stone was put up by King Harald (also called Harald Bluetooth) in the tenth century. It was in memory of his parents.

# WERE THERE ANY VIKING ARTISTS?

No pictures have been found from the Viking Age. But many Vikings carved designs into stone and wood. Many of the patterns are done in the 'gripping beast' design. When you look at the swirling patterns you can see animals gripping each other.

## ▶ THE OSBERG CARVINGS

**Archaeologists** found many woodcarvings on the Oseberg ship. There were four posts with animal heads, like the one on the right. The posts are all different. But each animal has a fierce look on its face. This was probably meant to scare off evil spirits. Carved sledges, a wagon and a bed were also found on the ship. Because wood rots, only a small amount of carving from Viking times has survived. It seems that farmers spent their spare time carving patterns when the weather was too bad to work.

## ◀ GOLD COINS

The iron axe on the far left was probably made for use on special occasions. A pattern has been cut into it and decorated with silver wire. Next to it is a silver brooch from Sweden. It was made around 940. The beast's paws grip the sides of the brooch in this simple gripping beast design.

Gripping beast brooch

## ▶ WOOD CARVING

These carved panels are on the wall of the church at Urnes in Norway. They were carved in the eleventh century. They stand for Yggdrasil, or the World Tree. The Vikings thought Yggdrasil held the universe together. Its branches reached the sky and covered the earth.

## ◀ JEWELLERY

The brooch on the left was probably used to fasten a woman's shawl. Rich people had jewellery made of gold or silver. Poorer people wore brooches made from cheaper metals. These brooches were sometimes covered in a layer of gilt or tin to make them look like gold or silver.

## ▶ STONE CARVING

The Vikings rarely carved pictures of people. This means that the cross in the drawing on the right is unusual. It was found in Yorkshire and shows a warrior from the tenth century. He is wearing a cone-shaped helmet. He has a sword, an axe, a knife and a spear.

**The Middleton Cross**

33

# DID THE VIKINGS WRITE BOOKS?

The Vikings were great storytellers and poets, but they didn't write books. One reason was that they did not have an alphabet like ours. They used **runes** instead. But the Vikings told stories and poems that were passed down from one generation to another. Many stories survived and were written down after the Viking Age.

## PICTURE STONES ▶

The Vikings enjoyed telling stories about the gods. Sometimes they carved these stories onto memorial stones. The stone on the right is from a story about Odin. The Vikings liked stories about Thor best. He got into fights with the Frost Giants (see page 26). Once he stole a jug of beer from the Frost Giants so that the gods could have a party!

## RUNES ▶

The Vikings only had sixteen letters in their alphabet. These letters were called runes. The early Vikings thought the runes were magic. They scratched them onto a sword to make it stronger. Later, the Vikings used runes for writing on memorial stones.

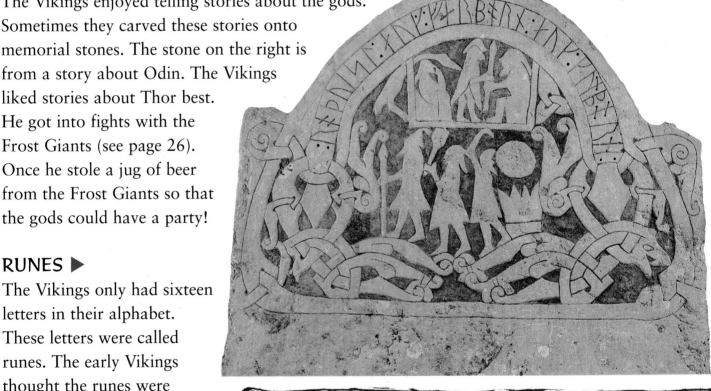

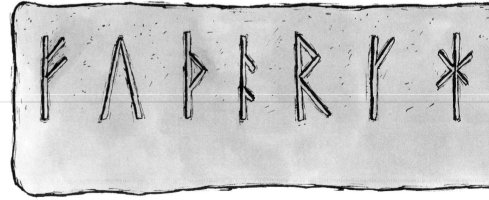

## POETRY ▶

The Vikings loved poetry. When they had a feast a poet was usually invited to tell poems after the meal. He would make up new poems or recite old ones. Some poets travelled round the country making up verses praising their hosts. If the host liked the verses, he gave the poet a generous gift, like this silver armlet. The most famous Viking poet was Egil Skallagrimsson. He once saved his life with a poem praising his enemy.

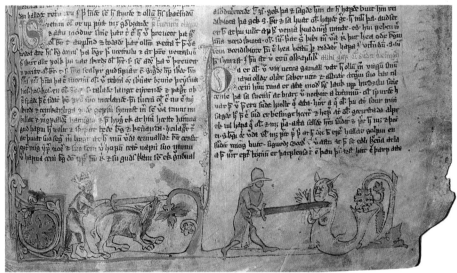

## 🔨 GOOD ADVICE 🦷

The Havamal was a Viking book. It was meant to have Odin's advice to the Vikings in it. He told them:

'Look carefully round doorways before you go in – you never know when an enemy might be there.'

'There is no better load a man can carry than much common sense – no worse a load than too much drink.'

## ▲ THE SAGAS

The Viking Sagas were legends written down in the thirteenth century. Many of them were adventures of Vikings who had moved from Norway to Iceland. Some of the books have little pictures in them. The pictures above show Olaf Tryggvason killing a wild boar and a sea ogress.

# HOW DID THE VIKINGS TRAVEL?

The Viking homelands were covered with marshes, lakes and mountains. This made it impossible to travel easily by land. Most Vikings lived near the sea and travelled by ship or boat. Their ships were made to sail on the open sea and in shallow water too. This meant that they could travel a long way inland on rivers.

## ▶ BUILDING A LONGSHIP

The trunk of an oak tree was used for the **keel** of the ship. Curved stems were nailed to each end of the keel. Wedge-shaped planks were then nailed to the keel. Each plank fitted over the next. Cross-beams were added to the inside. Then the **keelson** was fitted to hold up the mast and its sail.

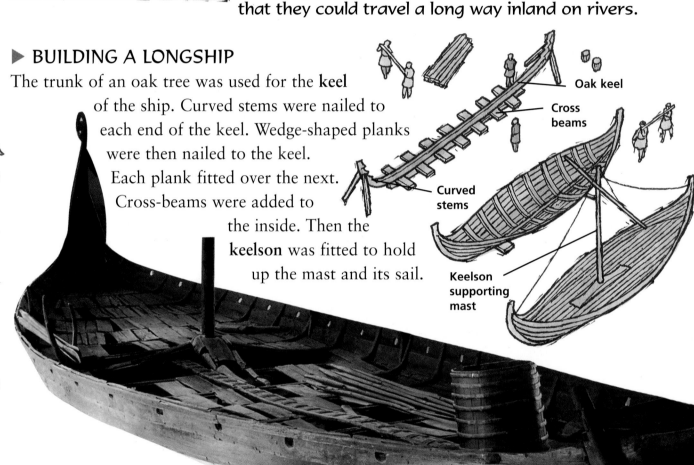

Oak keel

Cross beams

Curved stems

Keelson supporting mast

## ▲ THE OSEBERG SHIP

This ship was used for the burial at Oseberg in Norway. Earth had been piled over it. This had kept the air out and stopped the wood from rotting. It was buried in around 850. **Archaeologists** were able to repair it so that it now looks very much as it did in Viking times.

## THE OSEBERG WAGON ▶

This wooden wagon was found on the Oseberg ship. It belonged to a royal lady. It is covered in carvings. They tell the legend of Sigurd the Dragon-slayer. Most Viking wagons were made like this one, so that the body could be lifted off the wheels. Wagons used every day were much plainer.

### ▶ SHIP CARVINGS

This carved stone from Gotland shows a ship in full sail. The Vikings also rowed their ships.

Viking coins

### ◀ SHIPS ON COINS

We can work out how the sails and rigging worked on Viking ships by looking at pictures on coins.

 ### NAVIGATION

The Vikings liked to sail close to land if possible. On the open sea, they had to find their way by watching the sun and the stars. They had weathervanes on their ships. These had long streamers that blew in the direction of the wind.

# HOW FAR DID THE VIKINGS SAIL?

The Vikings were great adventurers. At first their journeys took them to the Faeroes, Shetlands and Orkneys. They then reached the coasts of Scotland, England, Wales and Ireland. Vikings from Norway settled in Iceland in 874. From there they sailed on to reach Greenland around 980.

## TRADE ▶

The **grave goods** buried with tradesmen tell **archaeologists** how far the Vikings travelled. These pots may have been brought back to Sweden from eastern Europe.

## ▼ TRADE

We can also see how far the Vikings travelled by the things that have been dug up in places where they settled. Enough pieces of wood were found in Newfoundland to make the reconstruction of this longboat.

## ▶ GREENLAND

This picture shows what is left of a Viking settlement in Greenland. Eirik the Red took people there around 985. The settlers from Iceland took animals with them on their ships. Because of the bad weather in Greenland, the Vikings eventually left their farms there.

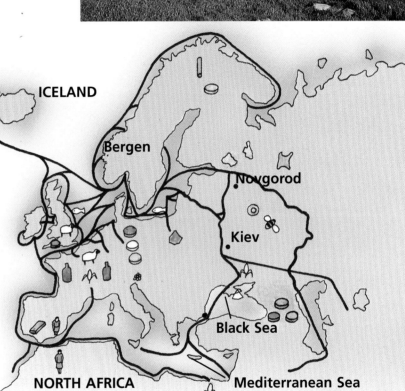

## ▶ TRADE ROUTES

By sailing along rivers, the Vikings could reach Arabia. They could get luxury goods there like silk and spices.

| | | | |
|---|---|---|---|
| ▮ Timber | ◆ Amber | ⬭ Copper | ✾ Spices |
| | ◁ Fish | ⬭ Tin | 🐑 Wool |
| ◖ Iron | ⋔ Corn | ⬭ Lead | 🍾 Wine |
| ✕ Furs | | 🧍 Slaves | |
| ✿ Honey | △ Salt | ▬ Silks | |
| ◎ Wax | ⬭ Silver | | |

ICELAND

Bergen

Novgorod

Kiev

Black Sea

NORTH AFRICA   Mediterranean Sea

## ▼ SILVER TREASURE

The silver Viking objects below were all found together in Lancashire. Many were **Anglo-Saxon**. Others came from Arabia and the continent of Europe.

## 🛢 TRAVEL PROBLEMS 🛢

At sea the ships of Viking traders might be wrecked in a storm. And on rivers there were **rapids** to get past. The Vikings did this by lifting their ships out of the water and putting them on wooden rollers. The ships could then be pushed overland and tipped back into the water on the other side of the rapids.

# DID THE VIKINGS HAVE AN ARMY?

The first Viking armies were small groups of warriors. They fought for themselves and not for their country. Later Vikings started to fight for their king. These armies were more organized. In 1016 the King of Denmark's army defeated the English at Ashingdon. This meant England had a Danish king.

## ▶ ▼ VIKING WARRIORS

Viking warriors protected their bodies with a shield and wore a helmet. Usually helmets were made of leather but some helmets were made of iron, like this one on the right. Helmets never had horns on them. The Lewis chessman below looks ready to fight on horseback. The Vikings usually rode to the battlefield where they then fought on foot.

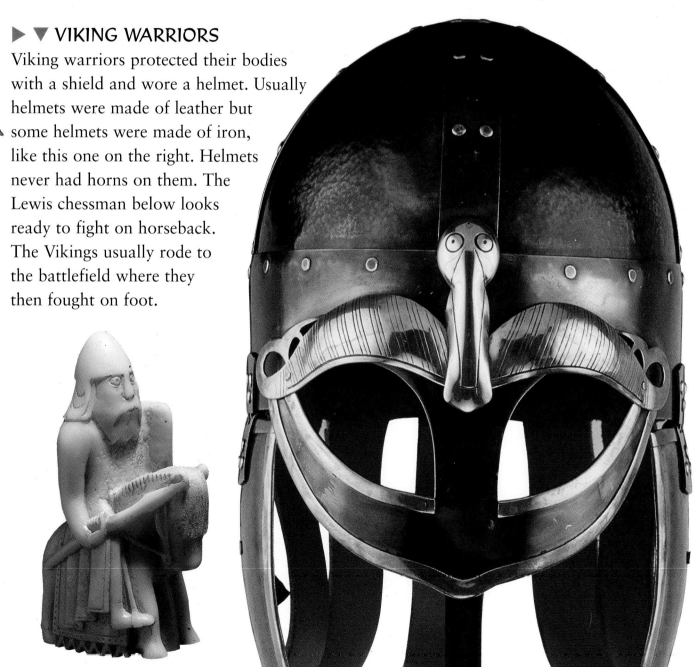

Sword

Battle axe

Shield

Spear

Scabbard

## ▲ WEAPONS

A Viking's favourite weapon was his sword. It was used to slash at the enemy rather than stab him. Vikings also used spears and battle-axes. Shields were made of wood and covered with leather.

## BATTLE TACTICS

Viking armies were never big so they had to take their enemy by surprise. If the enemy were winning, the Vikings fought from behind a wall of shields.

## DANISH BARRACKS ▶

The picture on the right is a model of a Viking site found in Denmark. The site may have been soldiers' **barracks**.

# WHAT HAPPENED TO THE VIKINGS?

The Viking Age was over by 1100. In places like Britain and Normandy the Vikings had made homes and married local women. In Scandinavia more land was being farmed. This meant that young men no longer went abroad to find farms of their own.

## ▶ WARFARE

In the eleventh century kings in Europe started building castles to defend their towns. At first the castles were built of wood. Later they were built of strong stone like this one in Kent. This made it much harder for the Vikings to come and attack the towns.

## ▼ AFTER THE VIKINGS

Stone carvers in England used Viking designs after 1100. These pillars are by the door of a church in Hertfordshire. They were carved in the late twelfth century. The carver used Viking gripping beasts and serpents in his design.

**Church door carvings**

## ▼ THE NORMANS

The Bayeux Tapestry is a long strip of embroidery. It tells the story of the Norman Conquest of England. In 1066, William, Duke of Normandy, became King of England. He was related to the famous Viking, Rollo. But the Normans did not live like Vikings. They spoke French and were Christians. Their soldiers wore coats of chain mail which you can see in the scene below.

## THE VIKING HERITAGE

Many English words that we use today were first used by the Vikings. These include sky, bread, egg, scrawny, snort and lump. Many place-names in Britain also come from the Viking Age. Names ending in 'wick' were markets. Names ending in 'by' were villages. And names ending in 'haven' were harbours. Another Viking word used in place-names is 'ness'. This means a headland.

# GLOSSARY

**AD**  The abbreviation of 'Anno Domini' used to show that a date is of the Christian era, which started with the birth of Christ.

**ANGLES**  People from northern Germany who settled in eastern and northern England in the fifth century AD.

**ANGLO-SAXON**  A member of one of the Germanic peoples, the Angles, the Saxons, and the Jutes, who settled in Britain in the fifth and sixth centuries.

**ARCHAEOLOGIST**  A scientist who makes a study of the remains of the past.

**BARRACKS**  A building where soldiers live together.

**BLACKSMITH**  A craftsman who forges and shapes iron with an anvil and hammer.

**CHIEFTAIN**  The leader of a tribe.

**CREMATE**  When someone's body is burned rather than being buried.

**DANGELD**  Money paid to the Vikings so they would go away and not attack.

**DIE**  A tool used for shaping metal.

**FRISIANS**  People from the Frisian Islands or Friesland.

**GRAVE GOODS**  Special objects buried with a body. Viking grave goods included food and often the Viking's sword.

**HARROW**  A frame of wood or iron with spikes, used to push the soil over freshly sown seeds.

**IRON ORE**  Rocks from which the metal iron can be taken out.

**JUTES**  People from north-west Germany who settled in south-east England in the fifth century AD.

**KEEL**  The part of a ship that goes from end to end and supports the ship.

**KEELSON**  The part of a ship supporting the mast.

**MONASTERIES**  Places where religious men called monks live and work.

**RAPIDS**  A part of a river where the current is very fast and strong.

**RECONSTRUCTION**  An object which has been made to look like the original.

**RUNES**  Stick-like letters of the alphabet, used by Scandinavians and Anglo-Saxons, that could be carved on stone, metal or wood.

**SACRIFICE**  A valuable offering made to please a god.

**THING**  The local meeting that decided Viking rules.

**TRADING CENTRES**  Towns where tradesmen and craftsmen sold their goods.

# INDEX